The God Exchange

Criss Cross

ARCHWAY
PUBLISHING

Archway Publishing books may be ordered through booksellers or by contacting:

Archway Publishing
1663 Liberty Drive
Bloomington, IN 47403
www.archwaypublishing.com
1 (888) 242-5904

Special thanks to Mike Nair for his art work.

ISBN: 978-1-4808-2052-4 (sc)
ISBN: 978-1-4808-2053-1 (e)

Library of Congress Control Number: 2015951709

Print information available on the last page.

Archway Publishing rev. date: 10/28/2015

Dedication

This book is dedicated to the memory of my longtime friend, Bob Hufman. Because of his brilliance and passion for God's creation and God's word, I gave him the honorary title of Dr. Bob. He was both my friend and co-worker in teaching for many years. I miss him very much.

Contents

Preface

The name of the department in the store has changed since I was a child, which was a long time ago. As I remember, at that time it was called the exchange department. The last time I was in a large store, I discovered that it is now called the service department. Returned items are taken there. I think the word *exchange* better explains what takes place in this department, but I understand that in today's business world customer friendliness is important.

Although the name has changed, the activity that takes place there is still the same as when I was a lad. It was a place in the store where you could take an item you had purchased, or that had been given to you as a gift, and for whatever reason, exchange it. You could exchange it for money or for another item of equal value. It was and still is a good idea.

I am not a person who likes to shop. As a child I learned to avoid it if at all possible. When I did have to go shopping, there were certain activities that my mother engaged in that produced in me a combination of being bored almost to death, and embarrassed far beyond death! Picture a 10-year-old boy standing in the ladies' hat department trying to look intelligent, while his mother and a few other ladies sit in front of several mirrors trying on hats. They are not trying on one or two, but maybe 20, 30, or more.

You're probably wondering why I didn't wander away and put a little distance between me and that embarrassing scene. That very good question has two good answers. One, home was about 20 miles away, and I did not want to ride home with an annoyed mother. Two, mom would ask me, "how do I look in this one?" I was not extremely smart as a young lad; however, I was smart enough not to tell her I really didn't know and that I really just wanted to get out of there. I discovered the word nice. "It looks nice," I would say, with some enthusiasm in my voice, as I tried to look interested for the moment. The near-death and embarrassment factor, along with sheer panic and terror, would multiply by a hundred if mom ever started toward the lingerie department!

Sometimes, when I went along, we would take something back to the exchange department. It was usually an item of clothing that didn't fit or was a wrong style or color. The lady in charge of the exchange department would usually ask why it was being exchanged or returned. The exchange was then completed.

Items then and now can be returned and exchanged for a variety of reasons.

☐ It doesn't fit.
☐ It's the wrong color.
☐ It's the wrong style.

☐ It has a broken part.

☐ Some parts are missing.

☐ The instructions are incomplete or too complicated to follow.

☐ I just don't like it.

Three years ago my wife and daughter-in-law went car shopping. They came home with a new car. The dealer told my wife to drive it for a few days. If we liked it, we could buy it. If for any reason we didn't like it, we could simply return it.

The ability to return and exchange anything we are dissatisfied with has become a part of our lives. If we are not completely, one hundred percent, totally happy and completely satisfied with something, there is no problem. We simply exchange what we are not happy with for something that we think will make us happy. This is a very convenient and very effective procedure for businesses, but it has created a big problem.

Here's the problem. Many people do this with God! Your first reaction is probably to say "Not me. I'm not sure that can even be done, and if it could be done I would never do it"! The apostle Paul told the people he was writing to in Romans 1:23 that some people had done exactly that. They had exchanged God for another god.

It's a puzzling and a frightening picture when you look at it. Imagine that people are lined up at the return and exchange department, with God in their shopping carts, waiting to exchange their God for another model. The lady in the exchange department is asking why God is being returned and exchanged. There are a variety of answers.

- [ ] This one clashes with my lifestyle.
- [ ] This one won't do what I want him to do.
- [ ] There must be something wrong with this one because he is so very slow.
- [ ] The owner's manual with this one is far too complicated and hard to understand; give me a god that is easier to understand.
- [ ] I have tried this God, and this is not what I think a god should be like.

There you have it. It's done. Practically, mentally, and spiritually the exchange is completed, and it's been done countless times over thousands of years. The reasons may vary slightly, but the thought is basically always the same. For many people God did not do or act or live up to the expectations of what they thought He should do or be. God did not do things the way they wanted them done, or when they wanted them done, or how they wanted them done.

As you read this book, be open to the possibility that you may be one of a very large group of people who have exchanged God for a god of much, much less value—a god that is in reality totally worthless!

Chapter 1

The God Box

ROMANS 1:18-22

The best place to start talking about the Bible, eternity, and God is with God himself. In the world today, almost everybody has an opinion about God. We hear things like God is dead, God is old, and God is acting Grandfatherly. Or maybe we have heard this. God is on vacation or is taking a long coffee break, or he just doesn't care about what's going on down here on earth anymore. Some people attribute things that happen in our world as being acts of God.

In addition, there is the realm of miracles and the supernatural. During the last few years, there seems to be an increase of interest in topics like Heaven, Hell, Satan, Armageddon, and the end of time and all things. There is a program on television that shows the earth after there are no humans left on the planet. I don't know where the people went. There are quite a few television programs, movies, magazines, books, and popular people expressing their view as to what Heaven will be like and what the requirements are to go to Heaven. Some of these people sound and act like they either own Heaven, are a major stockholder in it, or sit on Heaven's board of directors. The simple truth is that many people who express an opinion about Heaven and about the requirements needed to go there, are doing just that. They are expressing an opinion—a wrong opinion.

The first question that must be asked, discussed, and answered is this. Why do we even think there is a God? The answer is because of the God box within you! I know you're thinking that you don't have one. Think about it. Let's list the things you were born with that you had absolutely no choice in deciding if you wanted or not. Consider your head. Did you want a round one or a rectangle one or a square one? You had no choice in the shape of your head. Did you specify the color or thickness of hair you wanted or that you wanted straight or naturally curly hair? Mostly for men it is this thing called baldness. Were we given the choice of wanting to save money when we get older by not needing to go to the barbershop for a full haircut or just a trim, or did we want to have a full head of hair our entire life? Let's look at our eyes. Did you have a choice in the color or the spacing of the eyes, the eyelashes, and eyebrows? Did you choose to be nearsighted, farsighted, or have perfect vision?

Here is my favorite. If God had consulted me at the time of creation, this would have been my suggestion for improving mankind, and I'm sure God would have liked my idea. I would have said, "God, let's give human beings one more arm, with one more hand on the end of the arm." Instead of a matched pair, you'd have a matched trio. Come on. Admit it. I know you often have said, "I wish I had another hand." I would have suggested that God attach it in the center of the back and make it a little longer than the other two arms. I would have put an extra elbow and an extra wrist on it because it will need to be a little more flexible for what I want it to do. It would be called the center arm. You would have a right, center, and left arm. With the extra parts and length, it would have the ability to swing alongside your left hand or your right hand.

You're probably thinking, "I'm not sure this is a good idea. How would this be of any benefit to me?" Here we go. Pretend you're at a football game and your team has just scored the go-ahead touchdown. You want to clap your hands and scream victoriously. The problem is that the one hand is holding a five-dollar soft drink and all you can now do is scream. With my suggestion of an extra arm and hand, there is no problem. The center arm and hand would hold the soft drink and you could clap triumphantly. Ladies, sometimes you're busy cooking dinner and in one arm holding your baby. The baby starts to cry and wants to be fed. You're faced with either continuing to cook dinner for your hungry family and letting the baby starve, or letting your family starve and feeding the baby. With the center arm there is no problem. You hold the baby in your right arm and swing your center arm alongside your right hand to hold the bottle while your left hand continues to cook dinner. The possibilities are endless! Think how easy it would now be to scratch that unreachable spot on your back.

OK, let's go back to our list. You had no choice of when you were born. You had no choice of where you were born. You did not choose your mother or father or your sisters or brothers. You were not even asked if you wanted any at all, let alone how many. I sometimes think that I would like to be an only child born to billionaire parents. However, then I wouldn't have a younger brother to pick on and point my finger at when I got into trouble.

You did not get to pick your DNA composition. Look at yourself from the top of your head to the bottom of your feet and from the inside out. Now, let's be honest. We had no input into how we were made. We know we have a heart, lungs, and many other internal organs, because we can see them with medical equipment, and we know the important functions they perform. However, what about the things we can't see? What makes us laugh, makes us sad, or makes us love and care about certain things? We call them our emotions, and they come from our emotion boxes.

Call where they come from any name you want, but I think box works well. We can call it a happy box or a sad box because of how it makes us feel. Let's talk about the happy box. When we see something, our eyes tell our brain and our happy box, and if it's funny, we laugh.

We hear a funny story or joke and our ears tell our brain and our funny box, and we laugh.

Did you hear about the Texas teacher who was helping one of her kindergarten students put on his cowboy boots? He asked for her help and she could see why. Even with her pulling and him pushing, the little boots still didn't want to go on. Finally, when the second boot was on, and she had worked up a sweat, she almost cried when the little boy said, "Teacher, they're on the wrong feet." She looked and sure enough, they were on the wrong feet. It wasn't any easier pulling the boots off than it was putting them on. She managed to keep her cool as together they worked to get the boots back on, this time on the right feet. He then announced, "These aren't my boots." She bit her tongue rather than get right in his face and scream, "Why didn't you say so?" like she wanted to. So, once again she struggled to help him pull the ill-fitting boots off his little feet. They had no sooner gotten the boots off when he said to her, "They're my brother's boots. My mom makes me wear them." Now she didn't know if she should laugh or cry, but she mustered up the grace and the courage and once again wrestled the boots onto his feet. Helping him into his coat and hat, she asked, "Now, where are your mittens?" He said, "I stuffed them in the toe of my boots so I would not lose them!" Our funny box has been programmed by God. Certain things that we hear and see make us smile and laugh, and we feel better because humor is a part of our life.

God said in Proverbs 15:30, "A cheerful look brings joy to the heart, and good news gives health to the bones." Also in Proverbs 17:22, "A cheerful heart is good medicine." Our funny box, humor is a gift from God.

Now take the same logic and think about the God box. It should make us think about God. I can make my point about the God box in two ways. I can take the Bible and turn to Matthew 18:8-9 and read where it says you have two hands or feet or eyes, or I can make my point another way by simply looking at myself and other human beings. We have two hands, feet, and eyes. The God box can be proven in the same way. First take a look at all the different cultures, nations, and people, now and throughout time. There is almost always both a desire and a need to worship some god. The purpose of this book is not to explore other religions, but just to look at everyone's need for, and a desire to worship a god, to make my point about a God box.

Now let's look at what the Bible says about the God box. Romans 1:18-22 is a great place to study the God box. Its concept is really quite simple. When God created mankind, He put inside of him a desire to want to know Him. He also gave mankind the ability to understand that part of God so the desire could be fulfilled. God then put outside of mankind certain things that will clearly speak of God, so that mankind can clearly see and will have the ability to understand that they speak of God. Give every man and woman eyes to see and a God box program by God, and then place created things for their eyes to see that will say God!

It's not like it's extremely complex or hard to understand. I had to study algebra. That was hard. I had to study chemistry. That was hard. I had to study spelling. For me that was extremely hard. Twice in one verse, God says that He makes it plain to us. He created us, our God box, and programmed it so it responds to certain things in a certain way. When we see them, they say *God*. I like this. God makes it easy for us to grasp! These things outside of us that God created, that God wants us to see and that will tell us of Him, need to be really big and easy to see. Right? If He made them small and hard to find, we might miss them.

Here's what the Bible tells us they are—*all of creation*! That's too big for anyone to miss! It may be a different part of creation for each of us. For some people it may be a fantastic sunrise or sunset, both with sometimes utterly breathtaking displays of beauty. For some people it may be beautiful clouds. For others it may be fantastic mountains, the magnificence of the waves on the ocean, or the splendor of the autumn leaves when they turn from green to a rainbow of bright colors. Possibly it could be the rainbow itself. It was God's way of conveying a promise to his people, and it still says *God*. The rain says *God* and the sunshine says *God*. The clouds, mountains, rivers, oceans, plants, animals, and many other creations say *God*.

My God box responded to God's creation on a completely cloudless night. As I looked into the heavens, I saw an awesome display of stars shining brightly against a black night setting. I remember it very well. It said *God* and my reply was "Yes, there is a God." It was not a voice I heard with my ears. I heard it with my God box. All of mankind has a God box; all of mankind sees God's creation. This is one of those big things you don't want to miss. All of mankind knows there is a God. Romans 1:21 tells us "for although they knew God, they neither glorified him as God nor gave thanks to him." They exchanged him!

When your God box tells you there is a God, you have a choice to make. Choices are a great thing. We, in this great and wonderful United States, have a bazillion choices in almost everything we want. Ice cream is a good example. Forget your standard old flavors—chocolate, vanilla, strawberry, and combinations of those three. We now have Moose tracks, cookie dough, and even ice cream with candy bars crushed and mixed into it. Over the Christmas holidays we took some of our grandkids for ice cream cones. Guess what flavor one wanted? It was reindeer tracks—like, on Dasher, on Dancer, on Prancer, and Vixen. I asked him if he was sure that was a flavor. His reply was that he had eaten it before. Talk about feeling old. I can't even keep up with ice cream flavors. If you get an ice cream cone you don't like, it's no big deal. Just don't get the same flavor next time. There's a big difference between chocolate and vanilla. They look different, they smell different, and they taste different.

There's a very big difference between God and god. They look different, they smell different, and they taste diffcrent. The reward for the one we choose to follow and serve is also very different. When we hear a funny story, God has so programmed our funny box so that we laugh and we feel good. When we make the correct choice about God, God has programmed our God box to respond in a certain way. The correct choice about God produces in us a sense of joy that can come only from Him. It's a joy that is with us in this temporal life and extends into eternity.

THE FUNNEL

All pass through it into

Eternity

Heaven   Hell

Chapter 2

The Funnel

ECCLESIASTES 3:2

Five seconds seems like too short a period of time for anything of any significance or importance to happen, but it is truly amazing and frightening when you think about what can happen in 5 seconds. The list of things that a person can do in 5 seconds is hardly worth considering—a few beats of the heart, a deep breath or two, a good long sneeze, a short drink of water, or the entrance into eternity! Or maybe it could be a person driving a car, who has stopped at the stop sign, but does not see the young man with a loving wife and children and pulls out in front of him.

I have spent a lot of time on that road because it is a road that I have lived on for almost 60 years now. The curve is not really a very sharp one, and the crossroad is clearly marked. The list of things on the young man's mind on this Sunday were probably very similar to what any young man would have been thinking about. He could have been thinking about going to work on Monday, with its problems and challenges, or maybe when he would get time to finish painting the deck. There was also the need to start cutting a supply of wood for the winter. One of the cars needed new tires and a tune-up, and then there was the expense of the kids starting back to school. His thoughts were interrupted by a request from his wife. She needed a few things from the store for the picnic they were going to that evening. Would he be a "sweetie" and pick them up for her right away?

Although it interrupted what he was working on, it was a very welcome request. It was a very beautiful summer afternoon. This would also give him an opportunity to get points with his wife (that's a man thing), please her, and go for a ride on his motorcycle. He really liked riding his motorcycle, but lately had not had the time to do so often. This was great! He had lived on that road for many years and had traveled it often. We were both very familiar with the road, its curves, its intersections, and its slopes. It was a great day for a ride. It wasn't extremely hot and there was very little traffic, giving him a chance to relax and just clear his brain.

He made the purchases and started the 20-minute trip home. The road has all the things that make for a fantastic ride—a mixture of old and new homes all beautifully maintained, a number of farms, equally well maintained, fields with their gentle contours, and the corn and grass all a healthy bright green. In the fall when the leaves turn from green to a variety of dazzling reds, oranges, and yellows, people drive from distant places to see the amazing and spectacular scenery along this road. The road has a few gentle curves. It was built to bring roads closer to people's homes and farms at a time when a car's top speed was probably 30-35 mph. The road had been repaved and widened, but the curves were still there. The road makes a gentle bend through a wooded area and then goes straight to the crossroads, where a large barn is on one side. Then it makes another gentle bend.

My wife and I passed the accident just minutes after it happened. At that time we did not know who was involved, but it was obvious that someone had died. Many times I have looked at my watch and timed how long it takes from the curve to the crossroads. It takes about 5 seconds. Five seconds doesn't seem like a long enough period of time for so much to happen, but it's enough time for a person's life to end, a wife to become a widow, children to lose their father, relatives to lose a loved one, and many people to lose a friend. Sometimes the door to eternity opens very quickly and without much warning.

His last name started with the same letter of the alphabet as mine. So from ninth grade through twelfth grade, he sat either next to me or in front of me. We were not what you would call close, just friends. As the years passed, when we did see each other we would smile and wave and sometimes speak briefly about business or things that were happening in our lives. He died last week.

My first encounter with death that I can even vaguely remember was when my grandmother on my dad's side of the family died. She had the kindest, sweetest smile and the most wonderful warm personality of any lady I have ever known, other than my wife. As a young boy, my Sunday afternoons were very special and a lot of fun because they were spent on my grandparents' farm. My dad had a lot of brothers and sisters, so there were many cousins who could play with me. We played some great games.

One of my favorites was called "Fox in the morning." The game was played on a flat field, or as flat as could be found on a somewhat hilly farm. The game started with two teams separated by 50 to 60 feet with just one person being the fox. Everyone else went to the other end of the field and became the chickens. The game officially began when the lone fox would call out "fox in the morning." The large group of chickens would reply, "The chickens are ready." The fox's next response was "how many are there"? The chickens' reply was "more than you can catch," and the chase was on. The chickens left the safety of the roost and ran as fast as they could to the other side. The goal of the fox was to catch as many chickens as possible and thus add them to his team. To be the last chicken caught was a great honor.

My grandmother's sweet smile seemed even sweeter when it was still a long time until dinner and I was near starvation. She would make me butter and cheese crackers in whatever quantity was required to keep me from starving. A few years later my parents bought that farm and we moved into the farmhouse with her and my grandfather. She continued to show kindness to me in so many ways. I always thought that I was her favorite grandchild, but I'm sure the other grandchildren felt the same way. She was that type of grandma.

I don't remember the details of her brief illness because I was younger, and older people weren't supposed to get really sick. That sort of stuff, getting sick, was just for kids. As I remember, she had hurt her thumb in one of the double swinging doors in the farmhouse, and it was not healing properly. My dad and my uncle tried to convince her to go to the doctor. That was the only time I can remember that she did not have that sweet smile on her face. It was quite alarming and upsetting to me to see that her face showed pain and sadness. That was the last time I saw her alive. In those days children were not allowed into hospital rooms, so we had to sit in the waiting area. I heard my parents talking, but it didn't make much sense to me. Grown-ups weren't supposed to get sick.

In a few days we went to our church. I didn't understand what the word *funeral* meant. When we got to our small church, most of my relatives were already there or just arriving. Something was different. People were dressed up in suits and Sunday dresses. Many people were crying, which is something I thought only children did. I walked into the church, went to the front, and saw what was probably the strangest sight I had ever seen to that point in my young life. I had not seen her for a few weeks, but I knew it was my grandma. She was neither smiling nor sad, and she was lying very still. I went with my parents to the pew and sat down.

My first encounter with death was over. I sat in the pews surrounded by people who were sad and crying. I could not comprehend completely what was happening, but as I looked at that strange sight of my grandmother, I was confused and saddened because something inside of me knew I would never again see that sweet, kind, smiling face or have her prepare butter crackers just for me. I found out later when I was older that she had cancer, and that is why the thumb did not heal. There is that 5 seconds when you don't have cancer and then you do.

From the death of my grandmother until now, death has become an unwanted and certainly disliked part of my life. At the time of this writing, death has taken both of my parents, all of my aunts and uncles, and some of my cousins. It has also taken both of my wife's parents. Death has claimed many friends, classmates, coworkers, supervisors, and members of my Sunday school class.

One of the most difficult things I have experienced thus far in my life was the death of a young boy that I knew. He was a farm boy who was about 14 years old. He and our youngest son were great friends. He spent time with our son at our house, and our son spent time with him at his house. We knew the family very well and considered them good friends. His family attended the same church where I taught the youth group as well as a young believers class on Wednesday evenings. Following the class the chairs and tables needed to be taken down and put away. Although the boy was not a member of this class, he often came by to help me.

Once a year our church had a fun day as an outreach in the community. We had a lot of activities and events of interest to people of all ages. One time I used my dad's small fishing boat to give boat rides on a small lake near the church. Only a few people came for rides, but he came several times. He may have sensed my disappointment in having so few riders. He was that type of boy.

The things we humans have on our minds when we get up in the morning usually don't include any bad stuff. I often call this the *heaven syndrome*. We have the desire for everything in our day to go well or be very close to perfect. I am sure that teenager did not have an accident on his mind when he got out of bed that morning. He lived on a dairy farm. Dairy cows need to be fed if they are expected to produce milk. One of the lad's jobs in the morning before school was to take the tractor and wagon out to the field and cut some fresh grass for the cows to eat. He would then take the loaded wagon to the field where the cows were and unload the grass for them to eat.

The wagon had two rotating bars across the front with metal teeth welded onto them to put the grass on a conveyor that took it off the wagon and placed it on the ground. However, sometimes this smooth process would be halted by a stubborn large clump of grass getting caught in the bars or teeth. The simple fix was to stop the tractor, turn off the rotating bars, teeth, and conveyor, and dislodge the clump of grass. If the operator was running a little late, he would stop the tractor without turning off the rotating bars and teeth on the wagon, and just kick the clump of grass with his foot. It is truly amazing what can happen in 5 seconds—sometimes not what we plan.

About an hour after the accident, we received a telephone call informing us that when the boy had used his foot to dislodge the grass, his pant leg had gotten caught in the teeth. His leg was broken in several places. Normally, that should not be a problem for a young, strong farm boy. In the next telephone call, we learned that the accident was more serious than first thought. We were told that his leg was greatly damaged and might have to be amputated. The church was in constant prayer as were my family and I. As the days lengthened into weeks, he was transferred to another hospital, one that had more experience dealing with this type of injury. Although the very best technology and the finest doctors available tried to save the boy's leg, the decision was finally and reluctantly made to amputate the leg.

Soon after the surgery, the boy came home and was back in church. As he and I talked that Sunday, he seemed in excellent spirits. When we finished talking, he headed across the gym and out the door, on his one leg and crutches. I marveled at how great he looked, how fast he moved, and how well he seemed to be adjusting. I was certain he would have no trouble adjusting to living the rest of his life with only one leg. I was wrong. The next time I saw him was in his casket at the funeral viewing, several days later. From what we were told, the prolonged treatment of trying to save his leg had put him in a weakened condition, and a minor infection took his life.

I have read that there is a chemical in your brain that reacts to certain external activities and that it imprints images in your memory. The greater the external events, the deeper it is imprinted into your memory. I guess my brain must have released a gallon of that chemical that night, because I can still see everything in remarkable detail. I made the trip to the funeral home with my wife and four children with each of us holding back an individual dam of emotion. Once we were inside the funeral home and could see the coffin, six dams broke. Two adults and four children, all in tears, walked up to the coffin where we said goodbye. We knew our goodbye would be for only a short time, because we knew we would see him in Heaven.

The first time I heard him speak was when we started attending a new church. He was the teacher of an adult Sunday school class that was studying the universe. His passion and knowledge of that subject were amazing. He and I, along with our wives, became close friends. We served on many church boards and Christian school boards together. His desire to know more about our universe never stopped. He continually read and studied about God's creation, humans, our world, and the universe. The four of us spent many great and fun-filled times together. He was my co-teacher for many years and did an absolutely superb job. After class one Sunday, he told me about his recent visit to the eye doctor. The doctor told him he had a remarkably healthy pair of eyes. Several weeks before that, he had had his ears cleaned and told me he could hear better now than he had in years. The week after his visit to the eye doctor, he left his home in the morning to attend a meeting. He kissed his wife and told her that he loved her and the kids more than ever. Several hours later, while talking to his wife on his cell phone and telling her he was not feeling well, he suffered a fatal heart attack. Five seconds. I will see him in Heaven also, but for now I miss him immensely.

Our view of death is interesting. We all know that we're going to die, but we also all think that it's not going to be to-day, and probably not tomorrow, and probably not next week. It's one of those things that we know is going to happen, but we hope that it will be sometime in the distant future. When someone does die, we have come up with phrases and indirect ways of handling the topic. We say people have passed, they fought bravely, they've crossed over, or they rest from their struggle. It does not matter what your view of the Bible is, on the subject of death, most people will not disagree with Ecclesiastes 3:2. It states that there is a time to be born and a time to die.

The writer of Psalms 89:48 asks a question to make us think about the reality of death. What man or woman cannot see death or save themselves from the power of the grave? It states a simple truth in the form of a question with an implied answer. Not a single person. The truth that the Bible teaches about death is this: if you were born, you will die. You do not know the length of your life or the time when you will die. You may live a long life or a relatively short life. However, at some point this life as you now know it will cease. Life on earth is a very brief period of time. When it ends, a never-ending period of time begins. This is called eternity. The Bible also teaches that there are only two places to spend eternity—in Heaven or in Hell. Once you are in either place, there is no leaving one place to go to the other. Life on earth is a brief period of time to choose where we will spend eternity. Death then becomes a funnel through which all people, of all times, will pass from this short life into a time without end called eternity.

Chapter 3

Classroom Time Followed by a Lifetime of Learning

PSALM 89:15

I never liked spelling class. Out of 20 spelling words, I would get about 11 correct and 9 wrong. That was on a good day. If I missed more than five words, I would spend my recesses writing each word I had missed 15 times. The test was given on Wednesday, Thursday, and Friday; so on Wednesday, Thursday, and Friday afternoons I was sitting at my desk writing missed words. I had some company. About 10 other students in my class usually joined me. On our refrigerator I have magnets given to me by friends. Those magnets proclaim me to be a member of the bad spellers' club. I also have an interesting sign on the refrigerator that claims you need only the first and last letters of a misspelled word to be correct and your brain can figure out the rest. I would have liked to have had that to show my spelling teacher. She probably would have made me write each word 20 times. It's not that I didn't try. It's not that I didn't study. I studied hard and tried to memorize the spelling of the words. It's just that I lack that ability. Having 10 other classmates in the room with me was a little comfort.

As the years have passed, my spelling has not improved, but I have learned that there are other areas at which I am really good. I think most people are a lot like me in this way. They are really good at some things, okay at others, and then there is spelling. Another area where I think we are all alike is that we all make mistakes. I could probably write a thick book on all the mistakes that I have made. Some of them were serious and costly, and some of them turned out to be rather amusing.

The one about my cousin and the old milk can cooler will do well to make my point. My cousin came to my dad's farm every summer to help with the work on the farm. He was a very intelligent boy, six years younger than I, and two years younger than my brother. The first few years he came to the farm, the three of us got along great. Then one year my cousin began to realize that he was very smart. He also began to learn how to get on the good side of our mom. The combination of the two resulted in a very long and trying year for my brother and me. "Why can't you boys be more like him?" became our mother's favorite expression. Because our patience was becoming exhausted, we decided that before the next summer we had to do something. We had from September until May to decide exactly what we wanted to do.

The plan.
We had eight months to decide what to do, but we put off thinking about it until about one week before his arrival. We formulated a plan, but did not execute it immediately because we hoped that maybe he had changed back, and was not the obnoxious person he had been the year before. My brother and I decided to give him a few days to see what eight months away had done to him. A few days after our cousin arrived on the farm, my brother and I agreed that he had indeed changed. He was worse! He was more aware of his superior intelligence and picked up right where he had left off with buttering up our mother. We knew that although he was smarter than my brother and I, he was not stronger. What my brother and I may have lacked in intelligence, we made up for in sheer strength. We were both very strong farm boys.

One week after our cousin's arrival at precisely 9:05 in the morning, we executed our plan. We grabbed our cousin

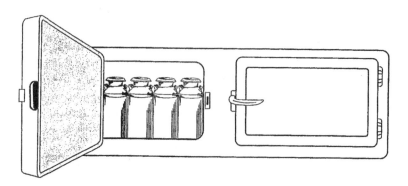

and stuffed him into the farm milk can cooler. We had carefully thought out the plan. My brother and I had practiced and timed the whole event several times to be sure it was correct. The milk can cooler had two doors, each of which opened only from the outside. Because four milk cans, each about 3 1/2 feet tall, could be placed in each side, there was more than enough room for one scrawny cousin. The ice cold refrigerated water was below a metal base on which the milk cans sat, in the bottom of the cooler. A pump supplied the ice cold water to two large metal assemblies above the milk cans. The assemblies had a series of holes that allowed the water to spray out onto the top of the cans. The milk cans, or obnoxious cousin, would not get wet until the pump was turned on. When the pump was turned on, it took 15 seconds for the pump to prime itself and pump water up into the metal assemblies above the milk cans. Another 15 seconds was required for the assemblies to be filled and begin to spray with any volume.

As I said, we had timed it many times. Our intent was not to soak our cousin; it was just to put him inside, shut the door, let him be in the cold darkness, hear the pump start up, and then hear the water start to reach the overhead spray assembly. Maybe if we timed it exactly right, we would let him feel just a few drops of ice-cold water spray. After all, if we soaked him, we would really be in trouble with mom! We turned on the pump and carefully watched the time. 5 seconds, 10 seconds, 15 seconds passed, and the pump was now primed. 20 seconds, 25 seconds, 30 seconds, and water was now in the overhead assemblies. At 35 seconds, drops were just starting to spray. It was now time to open the door and let our cousin out with only a few drops of ice-cold water on him.

As I opened the milk cooler door that morning, I had a very strange combination of feelings—a mixture of total surprise simultaneously combined with uncontrollable, hysterical laughter, with just a very faint touch of fear from what mom would say! We saw getting out of the cooler one totally, completely, ice-cold-water-running-off-him, not-a-dry-article-of-clothing-on-him, shivering cousin! He was too cold to talk. And the look on his face still makes me laugh today.

I was wrong. Although my brother and I had planned the whole operation carefully and timed it several times, we overlooked one small detail. Every time my brother and I had run the pump, it had been in the afternoon and the pump had not been turned on for several hours. When we initiated our plan to cool off our cousin, the pump had been turned on by our dad to cool the morning milk. Thus the pump had already been primed and the assemblies were full of water ready to spray. My cousin got 40 seconds of darkness combined with ice-cold water. My brother and I had made a mistake.

To be wrong about something and change that to a correct position should be an easy thing for humans, because we are wrong so often. If you're like me, that has been often. We know that sometimes it is not an easy thing to admit when we're wrong. To admit we are wrong sometimes involves other people. Who likes to think that a dearly loved parent, a trusted friend, or a teacher could have taught us something wrong? The really tough one is that no one wants to think that a religious leader, a former Sunday school teacher, or a pastor that we respect and look up to could possibly be wrong. Look, let's be honest with each other. We all make mistakes. I have made many mistakes. Some have been rather humorous; others have not been funny at all. Some have even been painful and costly.

My most serious mistake was when I started to realize that my understanding of God was faulty. That took place almost 40 years ago and was very painful. Using the Bible, I had to re-examine everything that I had learned to that point in my life about God. The unlearning and relearning have given me the most exciting, challenging, and rewarding adventure I have ever undertaken! To be wrong about something small may not be too difficult to admit and to correct. It's no big deal. As the size of the wrong increases and the amount of time I have thought wrong increases, it seems that the amount of effort needed to admit and correct the wrong really increases. By the time we get to something as big and important as God and eternity, some people simply refuse to even think about changing. It's like, if I am wrong about this, then I am wrong about eternity!

Probably the older we get and the more friends we have also add factors that make it more difficult to admit we're wrong and to make a change. We get into ruts, habits, routine ways of thinking and living. What would my friends think and say about me behind my back if I were to change my mind about this God deal? We learn in so many different

ways and have so many different teachers. We go to school
and have teachers, but we learn so very much outside a
structured classroom. We read newspapers, magazines, and
books. We listen to radio and watch television, and we have
friends who tell us what they think. Each day becomes a
new opportunity to learn. Life is a classroom in itself, and
the length of the class is lifelong. This book becomes an opportunity to learn and possibly challenge the thinking you
may have about God and eternity.

Let me challenge your thinking. What shape is this
object?

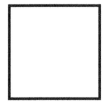

I'll bet you think it is a square, approximately 1" x 1". That
was easy. Right? What if I tell you that's not the correct answer, that you've made a mistake. What if by using the Bible
I can prove to you that the object is not what you think it
is, but that it's actually a circle. This is where the problem
begins. Everything that you've been taught, everything that
you know, tells you that the drawing is a square approximately 1 x 1 and that my suggestion that it is a circle is
completely wrong, even ridiculous. This is what took place
in my life approximately 40 years ago. Someone who became
my friend challenged my knowledge and understanding of
what I thought I knew about the Bible. I had been taught a

lot about the Bible, and I thought I knew a lot about God, what he wanted for my life, and about eternity. However, a great deal of what I knew was wrong, and I had to rediscover what shape the object was. It is my hope and prayer and the purpose of this book that as you read the following pages and chapters, you will allow the Bible itself to correctly identify the shape of the object.

Chapter 4

Zebras and Words

HEBREWS 13:8

There is a saying that zebras can't change their stripes. Zebras' striped pattern and colors have stayed basically the same since God created them. What they are born with they have their entire life. Words are different. Their meanings change from one time period to another. Sometimes a word can have two completely different meanings at the same time. It can be spelled the same and pronounced the same but have a different meaning! What I want to do now is show you how words have changed in just a short period of time.

I was in 11th grade and forced against my free will to study English. During that year one of our assignments was to write an essay on something we really disliked doing. The English teacher was an excellent teacher. Her effectiveness was showing up on my report card. The years before had seen grades of C and C −. These were now being replaced with B

and B+. I think I even flirted with an occasional A. As the
year moved on, I was not only becoming good with nouns,
pronouns, verbs, dangling participles, and other good English
stuff, but I was beginning to actually like and look forward
to the class.

I grew up on a small dairy farm, and there were several
things I could've written about. I chose the one I hated the
most, pulling weeds in the vegetable garden. With the time
it took to take care of the cows and other livestock plus the
crops of hay, oats, and corn, the weeds sometimes thought
we forgot about them. They began to think they owned the
garden, and that we really wanted them to grow instead of
the vegetables. They would grow thick, tall and fast. It seems
that if I pulled them out in the evening, the same size weeds
were back the next morning. It really seemed like that. Unless
one is an expert weed puller—and I was because of all the
practice I got—the job is more difficult than a person could
imagine. If you grasp a weed too high, it just tears off above
the root someplace and will grow back to full size in about
10 minutes. It must be grasped at ground level and pulled
slowly. If the weed is growing close to the vegetable plant, it
must be pulled slowly and precisely away from the vegetable
plant or the plant will be pulled up with the weed. That is not
a good thing.

My essay went into great detail of all this plus even more
on the subject. Let me set the scene. In English class everyone put their papers out on the table. In this class we sat at
very sturdy oak tables. Each table was long enough for eight
students, four on each side facing each other. Because they

were not individual desks, we could easily see the topics that several other people had chosen. It wasn't like we were cheating. The papers had been completed! The teacher asked the first student to go to the front of the class and read his essay.

As the first student began to read, the boy sitting across from me read the title of my essay "Pulling Weeds" and began to laugh. He tried to muffle it, but that made it sound even worse. The attention of the teacher and the whole class was now focused on the boy sitting across from me. Even the student reading in front of the class stopped. The teacher had a somewhat good sense of humor, but interrupting another student was well beyond her limits! She immediately went to the laughing student and sternly demanded an explanation for his disruptive behavior. Realizing the seriousness of the situation, the laughing boy composed himself. He apologized to the student who was reading, the class, and the angry teacher. The explanation for his uncontrolled laughter was interesting and amusing. This boy smoked cigarettes. In the late 1950s in this high school, smoking was prohibited and punished. Some of the boys and probably a few girls had found a few places where they could smoke a cigarette and not get caught. Because smoking at this time and in this school was a crime, it was given a code name. You guessed it. The code name was "pulling weeds." I think the teacher was somewhat amused by the boy's explanation. As I remember, she had just a trace of a smile for a moment on her face. Then the class continued. Zebras' stripes don't change, but the meaning of words does!

Let's take another easy one. The word is *gay*. When I was a teenager, if you had all your homework done, were getting

passing grades, and had a cute girlfriend, you were extremely
happy. If you had a girlfriend plus one of the other two, you
were probably just happy. On the other end of the emotional
yardstick was sad. Sadness could be brought about by quite
a number of things. The absence of a girlfriend was a major
contributor. Gay was like a slice of lunchmeat in your sand-
wich. One slice of bread was happy, and the other slice of
bread was sad. Gay was in the middle. It was how you felt
when you were not really too happy, but far from being sad.
I guess gay was how I felt when most of my homework was
done, I was passing in most of my classes, and any girl showed
a little interest in me. I am sure that was gay! The meaning
of the word gay has definitely changed from then until now.

Another word whose meaning has changed may come as
a surprise to you. It's an old word that has been around for
centuries. As soon as you read it, a meaning will immediately
come into your mind. The word in question is *Christian*. Do
you remember my discussion about squares and circles? My
purpose will be to show you what the Bible says the word truly
means. Ask a number of people about the word and you will
get many different answers as to what a Christian is, if they
think they are one, and why they think they are a Christian.
Let's make a list. A person is a Christian if he or she:

- Sings in a choir.
- Plays an instrument in a church group.
- Serves on one or more of the church boards.
- Teaches a Sunday school class.
- Is a pastor.

- Gives a sum of money to the church or some worthy charity.
- Has been baptized.
- Was dedicated as an infant.
- Has attended some membership classes.
- Is on the membership roll of a church.
- Attends church regularly, or somewhat regularly.
- Attends church on special occasions.
- Doesn't attend church but worships God outside of church.
- Believes there is a God.
- Has never done anything really bad, like murder someone or rob a bank.
- Is just as good or perhaps even a little better than most people who do go to church.
- Has tried to live a really good life.

This list could get quite long, depending on how many different people you ask the question. We live in an age when the original meaning of the word *Christian* has changed. It has changed because of a wide variety of reasons. To rediscover what the word *Christian* really meant when it was first used may require some special equipment.

Chapter 5

The Bulldozer

I t was a really neat place to go. They sold the best ice cream in town. I really liked to go into the freezer part of the building. When I was a kid, before television was even invented, almost nobody had a home freezer. The refrigerators at that time had a small freezer compartment that was only big enough to hold a half-gallon of ice cream and a few packages of frozen food. When you had a large amount of meat or vegetables to freeze, you took the items to this place and rented a place called a locker in which to store your frozen food. The freezer was a huge room with hundreds of metal boxes lined up in rows and built on top of each other. You rented a unit and had your own key. Going to the locker to retrieve your frozen food was fun, especially in the summer when it was hot outside. If you had been good, you might even get a big ice cream cone that at that time cost a nickel.

The same company that owned the ice cream and the locker plant also owned the huge building next to it. Milk was processed there, and then was bottled to be sold. They also made butter, powdered milk, and ice cream. However, as more and more people purchased freezers for their homes, the need for the locker plant ended, and that part of the business closed. Less expensive, but not quite as good, ice cream soon became available at other stores, thus ending the ice cream part of the business also. The building that contained the locker plant and where ice cream was sold also closed. After the other building had a fire that did considerable damage, the land and both buildings were sold. Two new buildings and businesses were to be built on the land. For several weeks, I ate my lunch across from where the two buildings were being demolished. The old buildings had to be torn down and completely removed before the new buildings could be started.

Because the buildings had been built with a lot of concrete, steel, and brick, the process of tearing them down was slow. There were several big machines being used to demolish and remove the old buildings. One machine swung a heavy steel ball into the building, knocking part of it down each time it hit the building. A bulldozer would push the demolished building material to a high-lift, which scooped it up and put it into a grinder. Trucks hauled ground-up parts of concrete brick-and-mortar away. In a remarkably short period of time, the old, unusable buildings were cleared by the bulldozer and his friends so work could begin on the new buildings. A bulldozer is a really neat machine. With a skilled operator at the controls, it can do an amazing amount of work and is almost unstoppable. It just moved steadily forward, day by day clearing the old rubble so the new buildings could be built.

Truth from the Bible has some very similar characteristics to the bulldozer. With God as the operator, truth is unstoppable. If you allow it to happen, the bulldozer named truth will clear away old and wrong ideas about what it is to be a Christian so you can begin to build new correct ideas. Jesus said in John 8:32 that truth has the power to set you free! Jesus was teaching the people that what they believed was wrong, and that wrong belief about Him was holding them captive. They had a choice to make. They could continue to believe what was wrong and be held captive by that wrong idea, or they could believe what Jesus was saying and be set free from the old wrong idea. You have the same choice.

The first time the word *Christian* was used was in the city of Antioch. We are told this in Acts 11:26. The meaning and origin of the word are interesting. History tells us that the people who lived in the town of Antioch prided themselves in coining words to describe persons and events. The first people who followed Christ called themselves believers because they believed Christ. They also referred to themselves as brothers and sisters because they were of God's family. They called themselves followers of the way because it was Christ's way they followed. They did not call themselves Christians. The nickname Christian was given to them by the people of Antioch.

I have always liked to give nicknames to people or things.

Most of my cars had nicknames. The Jeep I now drive to work is called Blackie. The Jeep I had before that was called Sporty. I always thought it was more fun in the mornings to say "Good morning, Blackie" than "Good morning, car." As kids, my brother, cousin, and I gave each other nicknames. When Linda and I started to have children, I gave all of them nicknames as they grew older. The oldest one was named Bobcat because he was so incredibly quick and fast. He could change directions instantly at full speed. Our second child was a girl whose nickname was Bear—you know, like a stuffed toy teddy bear. She was soft and cuddly. My dad gave a nickname to our third child, who was also a girl. I guess he heard me call the first two by their nicknames and decided he would nickname this one. The name he chose was Weasel. That's not a misprint. It was Weasel! That nickname is possibly part of the reason that I nicknamed our fourth child, a boy, the Bull. The third child seemed to have the ability to help her younger brother get into trouble, and the fourth child's reaction was sometimes a little stubborn. Weasel and Bull both got these traits from me. By the early teen years, both of these traits and nicknames were only childhood memories.

The people in the city of Antioch saw how "these" people lived their lives, saw how they worked, heard how they talked, and saw how they interacted with other people. After seeing some of their traits, they gave them the nickname Christians! The word has the meaning of those "belonging to Christ." Here is how I see it. They had a personal relationship with Christ that was so strong that they wanted to know what He taught, and then tried to live their lives according to that teaching. They really wanted to obey Him! The nickname Christian was not given as a compliment. It's not like the city people observed these people and said "They are so nice," "They are so wonderful," and "They are so great." The nickname actually was not nice at all. It was associated with hatred and persecution.

To be a Christian, when the word was first used, meant you loved Christ and knew and obeyed his teachings so well that other people could tell you were "one of them." They lived their lives like "Little Christs." The Bible tells us that we are born into God's family when we accept Jesus as our Savior. We then begin to take on the personality, traits, and desires of God, our new father. Just as human parents have children and those children have certain traits and characteristics of their parents, so do God's children. Remember that list that we compiled a little while back about what a Christian is. Let's add this one. As a Christian, I love Christ so much that I study His book, and as I learn what He wants me to do, I do it to the best of my ability. I hope by this time the bulldozer is starting to clear some wrong ideas.

Chapter 6

The *In* Group

The relationship that God wants with us, in my opinion, is really quite simple. Let me explain. On our farm we had about one acre of ground that had been a mess. We had done our best to keep the farm productive and looking attractive except for this one small piece of ground. It had many large rocks that were there from creation. Because they were there, the ground could not be farmed. Big rocks from the fields were drug into this area. With the passing of many years, thorn bushes, thistles, and weeds grew in abundance. It also had a small stream that flowed through it and over the years had turned it into a swamp. It was a mess! A well-traveled road passes right in front of it, and people driving on the road could see the mess.

Several years ago I decided to clean it up and make it look nice. I nicknamed this place my gym because it was where

I would go to work out. I went to the gym in the evenings when I came home from my job and on days when I was off of work. For 12 years, Linda and I had a small dog. His name was Hershey because he was the color of a Hershey chocolate bar. Most days when I went to work, Hershey went with me. My job requires traveling, and Hershey was great company and loved to be in the car with me. Almost every evening, weather permitting, Hershey and I would go to my gym. I would be breaking big rocks with a sledgehammer and carrying them to some low places. Some days I would cut brush and burn it. Some days moving ground and raking it was the plan for that day. Hershey spent most of the time walking around or sitting and watching. He had no idea what I was doing. I guess there were times he would sit and watch me and would think his master had slipped over the edge and was not acting intelligently. Here is a big and important point! Hershey did not understand what I was doing, but he still trusted and loved me! I loved him also, even when I knew he did not understand.

It is that way with God. The Bible states this in Isaiah 55:8, "My thoughts are not your thoughts, neither are your ways My ways, declares the Lord." Then in verse 9 he gives us an example of how far apart they are, "as the heavens are higher than the earth, so are my ways higher than your ways and my thoughts than your thoughts." That's not like the distance the Earth is from me when I'm on a ladder, or even up in a tall building, or even in an airplane! It's like thousands of miles. I may not know or understand what God is doing some or even most of the time, but he knows that and still loves me, kind of like with the dog! God loves you and me even when we do not know what he is doing and are confused by what we see him do! Jesus called his disciples friends in John 15:15. At that time they did not completely understand what He was doing, but it was very clear that He still loved them. Meeting Jesus and becoming part of His family is the most exciting and rewarding thing that anyone can do.

In is an interesting word. It's not very big, with only two letters. The dictionary gives it the meaning of "within the confines, primarily indicates possession, location, and condition." For example, if I'm outside of a house, then I'm definitely not *in* the house. I can stand outside the house and admire it, but I'm not *in* it. I see it, so I definitely know it exists, but knowing it is there does not put me *in* it. I can walk with other people and talk about the house, but I am still not *in* it. I could paint the house or make other repairs to the outside of the house, but I am still not *in* the house. When I was in my early 20s, there was a popular song that was a number one song for a few weeks. The music was great, but I think its popularity was in its appeal to the needs of a lot of people to belong to, or to be part of, something. Its title was "The In Group."

Jesus used the word *in* a lot. He used it to describe two different groups of people. John 12:37 tells us about the first group, a group that saw Jesus perform miraculous signs but still would not believe in him. John 12:42 describes another group of people that saw the same miraculous signs and believed in him. Each group of people saw the same miracles but made different choices. John 12:44 says that Jesus cried out, "When a man believes in Me, he does not believe in Me only, but in the One who sent Me." To believe in Jesus is to believe in God, the one who sent Him. One must also believe in His mission—His purpose in coming to earth—and believe in how He went about doing it.

It's like the house. I can believe there is a God, and I can believe there is a Jesus, but that belief does not put me *in* Him. I can believe He was born at Christmas and celebrate His birth, but I am still not *in* Him. I can believe He was a great teacher, a prophet who performed many miracles, but I am still not *in* him. To be *in* Jesus means I accept who Jesus is, His purpose in coming to earth, and the one who sent Him. There are many places in the Bible that state Jesus' reason for coming to earth. I like Luke 19:8-10 when Jesus was speaking to Zacchaeus. He said, "For the son of man came to seek and save what was lost."

Narrow is the road that leads to life and only a few find it.

Which road are you on?
Matthew 7:13-14

Broad is the road that leads to
destruction and many are on it.

Let's find out whom he came to seek and save. Romans 3:10-11 state that there is not one righteous person and that no one seeks God! That means that God does the seeking. It also means that there has never been, and never will be, a single person who will get to Heaven without accepting Jesus Christ's mission to save him or her! Here is a very important truth that the Bible makes clear. Jesus coming to the Earth and dying on the cross did not guarantee that everyone ever born goes to Heaven. That was God's part. You and I have our part. Luke 19:41 tells us of one of the times when Jesus wept. He saw a city filled with people who had rejected his mission and in so doing rejected Him. Jesus was so moved with sadness that He wept! If Jesus thought that His simply coming to earth and dying on a cross would save everyone, He would have had no reason to weep.

Your life, however long it may be, is a gift from God. He gives you this gift of life to learn of His mission and His love for you. Your life becomes your opportunity to make a choice to accept His mission and friendship, or reject both and exchange them for something and someone else. That opportunity ends at death. To most people the word *Heaven* itself conveys meaning of a place that is really nice—a place that is free from sickness, pain and health problems, getting older, and death. It's a place that will be free from wars and violence—free from earthquakes, storms, and other unpleasant things that we face now. Heaven is a place that will be simply beautiful, lovely, and very enjoyable. That's why almost everybody wants to go there.

Because everybody really has a desire to go to Heaven,

the teaching that Jesus presented to a crowd of people in Matthew 7:13-14 seems to be somewhat confusing. Jesus said, "Enter through the narrow gate. For wide is the gate and broad is the road that leads to destruction, and many enter through it. But small is the gate and narrow the road that leads to life, and only a few find it."

The Pennsylvania Turnpike is a major road near where we live. We travel on it several times throughout the year. In addition to access lanes to get on and off, the turnpike has two lanes in each direction and an additional lane when going up hills so trucks do not slow the flow of traffic. Thousands of people travel to their destinations on it every day. The bicycle road, by contrast, is known to only a few people. Its name was given to it by the people who live along it and have to travel on it. The road is so narrow that when two cars traveling toward each other meet, each must slow down and use the shoulder to pass. Very few people use the road because it connects no big towns and has no points of interest. When possible, it is avoided completely.

The point Jesus was making is easy to see when he used the example of the roads. Wide roads have easy access, few obstacles, are fast-moving, and have many travelers. Narrow roads are difficult to travel, have hills and curves, and have very few travelers. Spiritually, Jesus was giving a warning. He was asking people to look carefully at the choices they had made, and how they were living their lives. He was also saying that many people who thought they were on the road to Heaven were actually on the road to destruction. Why would people who really want to go to Heaven miss it completely?

One reason may be because of calluses. Confused? Follow my line of thought and Jesus' teaching.

When I was in the 7th grade, one of my classes was held in the sewing room and, no, I did not have to take sewing. At that time, it was not considered a skill that a boy needed or wanted. Thank you, school administrators! I felt punished enough with having to take several other required subjects. The room had sewing machines, long tables to cut material and dressers with scissors, pins, pincushions, and other sewing items. The girls used what was called a straight pin to hold material together and in place until it was sewn together. When the material was sewn together, the pins were no longer needed and some of them would accidentally fall onto the floor.

Of course, you realize that boys at this age are both adventurous and resourceful, and, as I remember, not completely convinced God knew what He was doing when He created girls! It was a very awkward time in our lives. Some days I thought that girls seemed to be wasting good air by even existing. Other days, I feared that maybe I needed a checkup by a doctor because girls suddenly had a very strange appeal. I guess it was on those days when they had the strange appeal, coupled with a total lack of knowing what to do about it, that the idea was born. A lot of the boys in my class, including myself, were farm boys, and we did a lot of manual work. This produced large muscles on our arms, legs, hands, and chest.

The work also produced a byproduct—rather large and somewhat hard calluses. I guess it was a desire to both impress the girls and gross them out that caused us to do it. We took the straight pins and put them through the calluses on our hands. We then closed our hands, approached the girls, opened our hands, and said "Hi" to the girls. At first this would gross them out. Calluses are a part of God's creation to protect the softer tissue from harm and are found mostly on hands and feet. Calluses have no nerves in them, so they are not sensitive to pain. Therefore, when the straight pins were put in them, we did not experience any pain. The girls did not know this at first. Calluses are good in some places but bad in others. They can cause a major problem when they form around the heart.

In Matthew 13:15 Jesus left the house He was staying in, and went to the lake and sat down. A large crowd of people came to hear Him speak. To make certain all the people could hear Him, He got into a boat and moved out into the lake a short distance and spoke to them from the boat. Jesus told his disciples that He was teaching the people this way because their hearts had become calloused. This statement by Jesus is terribly frightening! These people knew about calluses. Because most of their work was done by hand, they had calluses on them. Most of their traveling was done on foot, so they also had calluses on their feet. Jesus was taking their knowledge of the hardness and insensitivity of calluses on their hands and feet, and saying that their hearts had become the same way. Now this is big. The son of God, Jesus Christ, is teaching them, and they will not truly listen to gain understanding, because of the hardness and insensitivity of their hearts. Talk about exchanging a God for a god!

Jesus then told them what the effects of a calloused heart

had on people. They had ears that could hear normal everyday sounds and eyes that could see normal everyday sights. They just couldn't hear, or see, or understand, anything about God. Let's get a complete picture of their problem. Jesus was standing in a boat teaching them about God, but He was not the god they wanted. They had a different opinion of what a god should say, do, and look like. Their god would do things differently than how this God was doing them. They had an incorrect picture of what God was, and the calluses around their hearts were preventing them from accepting the teachings of God. They had over a period of years allowed their hearts to become calloused and insensitive to His teachings. God had to soften their calloused hearts before they could even receive his message of love, truth, and hope.

The Bible's teachings are just as true today as when Jesus spoke them. People allow calluses to build up around their hearts today, making them insensitive to the Bible's teachings.

Chapter 7

The Question

MATTHEW 16:26

Game shows are fun to watch and fun to play. You can be at home watching the television, playing a game along with the people on the television, and imagining that you are winning money and prizes also. There are some game shows that require little skill and little knowledge, just a lot of luck. I usually do pretty well with the games that start out with easy answers, unless the questions are in spelling or sewing. As the questions get harder, I usually do less well. Usually the farther along in the game, and the harder the questions get, the bigger the prize becomes. Some of the game shows have an energetic offstage announcer who talks about the prizes. With a voice infused with excitement, he describes the prizes as the biggest, the best, the top-of-the-line. If it's a trip he is describing, he will probably say something like this. "You will be enjoying two fun-filled, carefree weeks. While you are there, you will be staying at a fabulous four-star motel that has everything you could possibly want. It is a vacation dream of a lifetime, yours if you get the answer right!"

During the most important game that you will ever play, the prize for the correct answer will be awarded at the end of your life and will be bigger and grander than is possible to imagine now. An eternity spent in Heaven will be yours for the correct answer. You have reached this point in the game of life and the announcer with a voice full of love, hope, and excitement describes the prize you will receive for one correct answer. "You will be staying at the new and completely luxurious city of new Jerusalem. Some of its attractions include streets that are paved with pure gold, and a beautiful crystal clear river that flows down the middle of the golden street. The street is lined on both sides with rows of magnificently beautiful trees that have delicious fruit. The place you will be staying at is a mansion. It will have been designed by God. The interior design of your mansion has been done to reflect your personal likes and preferences. The foundation and walls of the city are constructed of valuable jewels and expensive material, and each of the gates to the city is crafted out of one big pearl. It's really hard to imagine the awesome beauty and splendor of this place." I'll try to describe the feeling that we will probably have when we first arrive at this city.

Times were a little tough and money was tight when I was a child, so I didn't get to go to a lot of places. I can remember this one time when we first arrived at an amusement park. I saw what seemed like hundreds of rides, a beautiful lake, and big tall shady trees. The smell of the delicious food was everywhere. Everything was clean and well painted. Lights flashed on and off, and everyone was happy. The thrilling, exciting, and happy feeling was heaven for me as a child. It was just completely wonderful to get there in the morning, to look around at everything, and to know that I had all day to enjoy it!

The announcer continues his description of Heaven. "As an added bonus, as long as you stay here in Heaven, there will be no more death or sadness or mourning or crying or pain! Because you see in this place, Heaven, the old order of things has passed away (Revelation 21:4). There will be no more headaches, backaches, leg aches, toe aches, finger aches, colds, flu, sore throats, fever, cancer, tumors, infection, brain problems, heart problems, lung problems, stomach problems, arthritis, broken bones, cuts, bruises, shots of any kind, tests of any kind, discomfort of any kind, no pain of any kind, or any other affliction. Those are all old order; they're not allowed in Heaven. No one gets sick or hurt or old and no one dies!!! All you have to do is answer one question correctly some time during your lifetime."

Because God wants you to get the answer correct, open Bibles are not only okay but are also recommended for this test. Let's review. First, there is a God; we proved that. Second, be careful of what you think words mean. Their meanings change, but the truths of the Bible don't. Base your answer on the Bible. Third, we all make mistakes, so that's no big deal as long as we correct them. Fourth, we use the truths of the Bible to clear away wrong ideas and construct correct ones. Fifth, Jesus loves you and gives you your life to make a correct choice about Him. Sixth, death ends your life and your opportunity to be *in* Christ, and your destination is eternally determined.

Let's prepare for the question. Turn to the book of Romans. If you're not familiar with the books of the Bible, there is a table of contents in the front of the Bible that will give you the page number of each book. The author, Paul, uses the first seven verses of chapter 1 to give his greeting to the people who would receive his letters. Then beginning with verse eight of chapter 1 and continuing all the way through to chapter 3, verse 22, Paul explains why every person who has ever lived has missed God's standard. God calls that sin. Romans 3:23 is a summation statement "for all have sinned and fall short of the glory of God."

Here is an explanation to help you understand correctly what this means. I have never robbed a bank, but I did, as a kid, tell the bus driver I had forgotten my nickel that was required to ride the bus. When I got off the bus, I went into a store, found my nickel, and bought some candy. You could get a big candy bar for a nickel back then. I robbed the bus driver! I sinned. You say a nickel is not a very big deal. I still took something that did not belong to me; it belonged to the bus driver. God calls that stealing, and he also calls it sin. I have been very happily married to Linda for over 45 years. Neither physically nor mentally have I ever been unfaithful to her. However, as a teenager before I met Linda I had a very colorful and active mind when it came to certain young and attractive girls. God calls that sin. Let me be very honest. When I look at God's standards and then look at my life, I have come up very short of His standards many, many times. In other words I have sinned many times. If you are honest with yourself, look at your life, and compare it to God's standards, you will also agree that the Bible is correct when it states that all of us have sinned.

You may be thinking that it's not a big deal. It was just a nickel, and I didn't even get close to the girls. I may have wanted to kill a few people in my life who made me angry, but I didn't. By my own admission, I have broken four of God's Ten Commandments! First, I lied to the bus driver, which made me a liar. Second, I stole money and that made me a thief. God says to think sexually about anyone other than the person of the opposite sex that I am married to is sin, so that's number three. To hate another person, a creation of God, so much that I want to end his or her life is murder. I'm guilty of that also—number four. That makes me a lying, lusting, murderous thief! God has a standard of righteousness that all people must meet. If we break God's law even one time, we alone can't meet that standard. We need help. We need someone to save us. That someone is Jesus. Are you still not convinced that one wrongdoing is serious? Is some of this really such a big deal that it would upset God? Remember the bulldozer? You may need it here to clear a wrong idea.

Was it really a big deal what the first couple did? All that Adam and Eve did was eat a piece of fruit from the one tree God told them to avoid. That's not even as bad as the nickel. The result of their one act, one sin, was enormous! They were driven out of their home, the Garden of Eden. They had to make a living by working the now cursed ground. Here is the biggie. Physical and spiritual death would now be a part of mankind's life. We will all die twice! Physical death and spiritual death were never part of Adam and Eve's life in the garden until the point when they sinned. Spiritual death took place the first time Adam and Eve disobeyed God, which brought separation from him. Physical death takes place later in life. The first part of Romans 6:23 tells us "for the wages of sin is death." Wages are what we have earned for something we have done. What we have done is disobeyed God. God calls that sin and tells us that the results of that sin, what we have earned, is death, both physical and spiritual.

We covered the physical death in the first chapter; we all know it will happen. We just don't know when and how, so we need to be ready. Spiritual death is separation from God. In Luke 16:19-31 Jesus tells what will happen to all individuals when they die. They will go to one of two places—Abraham's side, another name for Heaven, or Hell. The Bible clearly states that in Hell, there will be torment and agony. The person in Heaven will be in a place of comfort. It also states that it will be impossible to go from one place to another. Once in Heaven, one will always be in Heaven; once in Hell, one will always be in Hell! People decide where they go before they die. Death ends the time to make that choice.

The Bible clearly teaches that God takes sin seriously. We may think some sin is small, but to God it's all big and serious. God's love is also something that is very big and serious. Romans 5:8 tells us how big God's love is: "but God demonstrated his own love for us in this while we were still sinners, Christ died for us." This verse tells us that God showed us the great love He has for us when Jesus died on the cross. Jesus Christ was God's son. Like God He was perfect. He had no sin. He did not have to die. You only have to die if you sin, so why did He die? Because of His great love, He wanted to give you and me a gift.

I really like to give and to receive gifts. Christmas at our home is a great time. Usually most of the kids and grandkids are home, and we have a great time with each other. Opening the presents is fun and exciting. We all take turns, each opening a gift, telling who it is from, and expressing thanks to whoever gave it. God tells us about a gift He has for us. This gift is given to us by God, and it is eternal life, everlasting, without end. The last part of Romans 6:23 tells us "but the gift of God is eternal life in Christ Jesus our Lord." There's that word *in* again. It is the absolute greatest gift anyone could ever receive.

Romans 10:13 tells us how to receive this gift. "Everyone who calls on the name of the Lord will be saved." It may be bulldozer time again. To call on Jesus means that I believe in what his mission was, as it applies to me. I can believe Jesus was a good man, a great teacher, a prophet, celebrate his birth at Christmas, and do a lot of good things. However, to call on His name means that I know I am a sinner and that sin will separate me from God for eternity. To call on His name means I know His death on the cross was for me. I know that He died for me so that He could offer me the free gift of eternal life. To call on His name means I know I need a Savior, and He is the only one who can save me.

To call on simply means to talk; you talk to God the same

way that you talk to anyone else. Talking to God is called prayer. It always seems to me to be a question that should be really easy to answer. The game show host describes two places that you can go for a vacation. The one place is Heaven. He describes the other one with a different tone of voice. His voice is sad and less enthusiastic, yet very frank and honest. Hell is real. The Bible speaks of it often. Jesus warned people of its horrors repeatedly throughout the Bible. Jesus talked about both Heaven and Hell in Luke 16:19-31. Jesus described the condition of a man who died and went there with words like this. He was in torment! He was in agony in the fire.

He had all his senses, he could see, he could hear, he could talk, and he was thirsty but had no water. He still had a sound mind. Because he had a genuine concern for the family he had left behind, he was told that this was permanent and that he was without hope of ever leaving that horrible place.

Almost anybody who has any degree of intelligence would make the choice to go to Heaven, the nice place. Why would anybody want to go to a place like hell? If given the choice of going on a vacation to Hawaii or someplace that is really hot and nasty, where you will be miserable for

the entire vacation, most people would choose Hawaii. It's
your turn to choose. Are you ready for the most important
question you will ever answer? Do you want the gift of eternal
life in Heaven with Jesus? If you do, right now, wherever you
are, just bow your head, close your eyes, and pray this prayer.
"Dear Jesus, right now I know I have done things that you call
sin, and that sin has separated me from you. I know that you
died on the cross and paid the price for my sins, so you could
give me the gift of eternal life, in Heaven, with you. I ask you
to forgive my sins, help me to live the rest of my life for you,
and take me to heaven when I die."

I really hope you have prayed and asked Jesus to be your
Savior. It was the greatest thing I ever did! If you prayed and
asked Jesus to be your Savior, it will be the greatest thing you
will ever do. Expect some exciting changes to begin in your
life now that you have become one of His, because you are
in Him. He wants to become the very best friend that you
have. You should really want to know more about Jesus. That
means that you should regularly read and study His Word,
the Bible. God will want you to become involved in a group of
other Christians so you can learn more about Him and have
fellowship with other Christians. To find a church God wants
you to go to, simply ask Him to help you. Talk to God as you
would any other person. Say, "God, please help me find the
church you want me to go to; direct me to it."

If you did not pray and ask Jesus to save you, either you
have a problem or God has a problem. God did a really ex-
treme thing when He sent His son to earth to pay the penalty
for our sin debt by dying on the cross. Really, what more could

He have done to show you He loves you? He wrote a book to tell you how much He loves you. Have you ever read it? He created you in a very special way so you could recognize Him from everything that surrounds you.

God does not have the problem. People who reject Him do. The writer of Hebrews makes this statement in chapter 2:1: "We must pay more careful attention therefore, to what we have read, so that we do not drift away." The thought behind that statement is this. A lot of people go to Hell not because they actively oppose Jesus Christ. They may think very highly of Him. They go to Hell because they neglect Him and His message. It is as if they simply drift past His loving invitation. They know some things about Him, but they just don't have time or make the effort to take His message seriously. Some people just don't care, until it is too late.

Please don't be one of those people who are on the road to Hell, the road that is wide and leads to destruction.

Scripture Index

Made in the USA
Monee, IL
09 November 2021